BITS TO UPSC

RESEARCH TO REALISATION

SHUBHAM PAL SINGH

BookLeaf
Publishing

India | USA | UK

Made with ❤ on the BookLeaf Publishing Platform
www.bookleafpub.in
www.bookleafpub.com

Dedication

These poems are for everyone who has helped me on my journey. First, to the UPSC, for pushing me to learn and serve. To BITS Pilani, where I gained so much knowledge. To my father, Dr. Shashi Pal Singh, for his wise advice. To my mother, Beena Pal, for her endless love and support. To my wonderful wife, Shivi Singh, for always being there for me. And to my brother, Yash, and sister, Khushi, who bring so much happiness to my life. Thank you all for believing in me; your support is in every word.

Preface

This book is a chronicle of a journey, a tapestry woven from threads of education, experience, and the unwavering pursuit of a dream. It's a story of navigating the complexities of academic rigor at BITS Pilani, the pragmatic realities of work, the grounding influence of family, and the profound impact of spiritual guidance. From the halls of academia to the interview rooms of the UPSC, this narrative is a testament to the power of resilience, the importance of mentorship, and the transformative potential of focused intention. I share this journey not as a guide, but as an offering, hoping that within these pages, you may find resonance, inspiration, and perhaps, a spark to ignite your own path

Acknowledgements

I owe a debt of gratitude to the many individuals who have supported me on this journey. First and foremost, I thank my family for their unwavering love and encouragement. To Shri Dr. Rishi Mohan Bhatnagar Sir, thank you for your invaluable guidance and mentorship. I also extend my sincere appreciation to the faculty at BITS Pilani for their dedication to my education. Finally, thank you to everyone who believed in me and inspired me to pursue my dreams.

1. The Journey: Education, Experience, and Beyond

From humble starts, a journey's spun,
"My Early Education," where seeds begun.
Then "Work Experience," a path so wide,
Where skills were forged, and dreams applied.

"Family Contribution," love's gentle hand,
A steady base, in shifting sand.
"Two Mtechs," from BITS Pilani's grace,
A double delve, in knowledge's space.

"Dr. Bhatnagar's Guidance," a light so bright,
A mentor's wisdom, guiding the night.
"Spirituality's Focus," a peaceful art,
To center the mind, and play a focused part.

"Research Paper," and conferences' call,
Where insights shared, stood proud and tall.
"Guest Professor," at BITS' famed halls,
To share the knowledge, answering calls.

"First UPSC Interview," a venture bold,
A tale of nerves, and stories told.
"Second Interview," a lesson learned,
Where strength refined, and spirit burned.

"How to Apply," a guiding phrase,
To open doors, in future days.
A life of learning, reaching high,
A tapestry woven, 'neath life's vast sky.

2. From Average to Ascent: A Tale of Hard Work and Transformation

From shifting towns, a student's plight,
Bhopal, Delhi, bathed in changing light.
Ranchi's halls, where lessons grew,
"Hard work beats talent," a vision true.

A father's form, a disciplined grace,
Four a.m. prayers, a steady pace.
St. Francis's call, to citizens' might,
Polished manners, shining bright.

DAV's merit, a challenge met,
DPS, JVM, a hurdle set.
FIITJEE's fire, a burning quest,
A01's peak, where talents pressed

.

Shashi Shukla's brilliance, a rapid hand,
Abhijeet's climb, to serve the land.

A gap year's pause, a score's release,
SRM's halls, a mechanical peace.

Ninty four Dot five, a first semester's gleam,
Eight nine Dot one, a four-year dream.
Aptitude's shadow, a placement's sting,
Prashant's guidance, a hopeful spring.

MADE EASY's path, a GATE's embrace,
BITS Pilani's shores, a different space.
Networking's art, professors' aid,
A transformation, bravely made.

Mukherjee's lessons, a reasoning's key,
OnePlus's rounds, a victory.
Ninth in the test, first in the talk,
A hidden strength, on which to walk.

Mechatronics' depths, a knowledge gained,
Fracture, CAD, where skills were trained.
A journey's weave, through trials' fire,
Where hard-won lessons, dreams inspire.

3. From Design to AI: A Pursuit of Service

Hyderabad's lines, where pipelines took their form,
Mahathi's training, weathering life's first storm.
AutoCAD's precision, Caesar's measured might,
Sprinkler rings designed, in day and fading light.

A fifteen-thousand start, a thirty's tempting call,
But OnePlus beckoned, answering a different thrall.
Ashok's shared flat, a lockdown's silent sway,
Python's coded dance, where automation held sway.

Selection Post's whisper, a government's steady hand,
SSC's waitlist's shadow, on dreams within the sand.
Lava's rise, thirteen seminars' bright flame,
AI and learning's call, to carve a lasting name.

UPSC's interview, a driller's measured test,
Sixty-three's proud score, a heart put to the best.
One post's cruel edge, a waitlist's bitter sting,
Yet onward driven, where new aspirations sing.

TCS's AI embrace, a global stage unfurled,
Mexico's promise, a new and vibrant world.
Sixty thousand's lure, a tempting, foreign shore,
But UPSC's calling, a dream to still explore.

From pipelines' design, to AI's boundless reach,
A journey's winding path, where higher goals beseech.
A driven soul's pursuit, a gazetted officer's plea,
Where service's calling, sets a spirit truly free.

Generate Audio Overview

4. The Guiding Stars

A father's wisdom, a steady hand,
Through B.Tech's trials, a guiding strand.
GATE's sharp corners, M.Tech's deep dive,
UPSC's summit, where dreams survive.

A mother's comfort, a gentle grace,
Nourishing spirit, in time and space.
From simple meals, to whispered praise,
A love that strengthens, through all my days.

A wife's devotion, a tender art,
A home's warm haven, a brand new start.
Through interview's stress, and tasks untold,
A steady presence, more precious than gold.

A brother's keen eye, a sister's bright aid,
Through research papers, their support displayed.
A family's circle, a bond so strong,
Where love's true melody, echoes along.

These guiding stars, that light my way,
A debt of gratitude, I can never repay.
Each loving gesture, a whispered plea,
"Thank you, family, for believing in me.

5. BITS: A Coder's Journey

In 'seventeen, the GATE's call did sound,
A quest for knowledge, on hallowed ground.
Six hundred three, a score so bright,
Pilani's gates, bathed in learning's light.

A double stipend, a student's grace,
MHRD's aid, a helping space.
Teaching's wisdom, a shared embrace,
Pilani's growth, in time and place.

Kulkarni's doubts, dispelled with care,
Patil's resume, a polished flair.
Mouli's mocks, with companies' might,
GE's challenge, in fading light.

OnePlus's realm, a brief sojourn,
Software's gap, a lesson to learn.
Pilani's halls, a second climb,
Ravi Kumar's guidance, transcending time.

Bera's industry, a sharpened view,
Thesis refined, honest and true.
"AI Image Forgery," a deep dive's art,
CNN's power, a brand new start.

Soft Architecture's peak, a perfect score,
Agile's depths, to learn and explore.
TCS's call, in cloud's domain,
Pilani's path, a fruitful gain.

From GATE's first step, to AI's embrace,
BITS Pilani's mark, in time and space.
A journey shaped, by knowledge's flame,
A coder's story, etched in its name.

6. The Mentor's Light

November's chill, a meeting's start,
Dr. Bhatnagar's wisdom, set apart.
Lava's helm, with visions grand,
Tech Mahindra's heights, a guiding hand.

Ankitgram's heart, a service's plea,
AA2IT's dawn, for all to see.
Bhartiya Shiksha, a guiding star,
A mentor's path, reaching afar.

Thesis's thread, a research's quest,
"419's error," put to the test.
"Dblocks' depths," optimized with grace,
Knowledge's bloom, in time and space.

Chitra Vihar's walls, a counsel's gleam,
Hyatt's halls, where papers stream.
A book's idea, a spark so bright,
Igniting thoughts, in darkest night.

VIVIBHA's stage, a wisdom's call,
Delhi's halls, where lectures enthrall.
Scientific thought, a guiding creed,
Confidence sown, a fruitful seed.

Patent's promise, wealth's grand design,
IPO's ascent, a future's shine.
Navratra's grace, a bond so deep,
Gratitude's song, the heart will keep.

A mentor's light, a guiding ray,
Illuminating, a brighter day.
For insightful words, and wisdom's art,
Dr. Bhatnagar's grace, within my heart.

7. The Forged Image's Shadowed Frame

In realms of pixels, where truths reside,
A digital canvas, where secrets hide.
"Image Forgery," a challenge deep,
Where real and false, their shadows keep.

Deep learning's lens, a watchful eye,
Through neural networks, where patterns lie.
CNN's power, a searching gaze,
To pierce the veil, through digital haze.

Eight weeks' labor, a focused stride,
A white paper's truth, where facts abide.
Technical craft, with thought's keen art,
A rational mind, to play its part.

Five stars gleam, on knowledge's stage,
Creative thought, to turn the page.
Report's structure, a clear design,
Significance shown, where insights align.

"References sought," the evaluator's plea,
A final touch, for all to see.
"Good" the grade,a well-earned praise,
For efforts shown, in countless ways.

Ravi Kumar's guidance, a steady hand,
Through coded depths, to understand.
And to the AI, that helped to weave,
This summary's form, where truths believe.

From forged illusion, to clarity's light,
Deep learning's triumph, in digital night.
A student's journey, in code's embrace,
To find the truth, in time and space.

8. The Soul's Serene Ascent

B.Tech's close, a lonely tide,
GATE's looming shadow, where doubts reside.
Stress's grip, a spirit's plight,
Seeking solace, in fading light.

Art of Living's gentle sway,
ISKCON's wisdom,to light the way.
"Subconscious Power," a guiding hand,
To find the strength, to understand.

Hanuman's chant, at morning's grace,
Confidence blooms, in sacred space.
Temple's silence, a peaceful hour,
Prayers ascend, with gentle power.

Gita's wisdom, "Nishkam's" call,
Selfless action, to stand up tall.
Mahabharat's war, Ramayan's tale,
Moral lessons, that will not fail.

"Dharma's decline," a verse's plea,
"I manifest," for all to see.
"Soul's eternal," a tranquil thought,
By fire untouched, by water unbought.

Rishikesh's Ganga, a cleansing flow,
Mussoorie's peaks, where spirits grow.
Prayagraj's Kumbh, a holy dip,
Cleansing sins, from heart and lip.

Kurukshetra's fields, where Krishna spoke,
Brahma Sarovar's peace, a sacred stroke.
Baan Ganga's shore, where Bhishma lay,
Spiritual grace, to light the way.

From lonely depths, to serene ascent,
A soul's rebirth, divinely sent.
Through faith and prayer,a peaceful mind,
A spiritual journey, for all mankind.

9. VIVIBHA's Scholar's Light

November's days, in Delhi's heart,
Research's call, a brand new start.
Five thousand minds, a vibrant throng,
Where scholars met, and wisdom strong.

SGT's halls, a welcoming space,
Hostels' warmth, a shared embrace.
With Maurya's wisdom, Gupta's keen mind,
Knowledge's seeds, for all to find.

Breakfast's spread, a diverse array,
Bhagwat's voice, to start the day.
"Knowledge Science," Reddy's wise word,
Sitharam's vision, clearly heard.

Space's vast reach, and rockets' flight,
Guidance sought, in learning's light.
Sahasrabudhe's grace, a blessing's hand,
In scholar's quest, across the land.

Yoga's calm, with Ramdev's sway,
"Industry's link," a brighter day.
Ahuja's insight,China's keen view,
Kamble's wisdom, ever true.

Pradhan Ji's presence, Bhatnagar Ji's grace,
"Research to Realisation," in this place.
Trophies gleam, and shawls bestowed,
VIVIBHA's vision, brightly showed.

A scholar's journey, in knowledge's tide,
Where minds converge, and truths abide.
From forged images, to wisdom's art,
A conference's spark, within the heart.

10. From Alumnus to Professor: A BITS Pilani Story

A hall of echoes, Pilani's grace,
Where learning's spirit finds its place.
A guest returned, with knowledge deep,
Conversational AI, secrets to keep.

Quizzes and exams, a scholar's hand,
Grading assignments, across the land.
"Advanced Rag," a tale to spin,
Where wit and wisdom intertwine within.

Seventy thousand, a token's due,
But richer still, the lessons true.
Students' voices, sharp and bright,
Challenging scores, with all their might.

Wave diagrams drawn, equations clear,
A spirited debate, banishing fear.

Two marks reclaimed, a victory won,
The BITSian spirit, brightly spun.

A missing link, a playful plea,
"Consider us, sir, just this time, see?"
Then, in the end, the link did appear,
Resourcefulness shown, banishing fear.

Architecture, OOAD's design,
Agile's swift flow, where truths align.
A hundred percent, a shining star,
A path to teach, both near and far.

Rao, Ravi Kumar, Bhagat's guide,
Kulkarni's wisdom, side by side.
Gratitude's echo, soft and low,
For seeds of knowledge, they helped to sow.

11. First UPSC Interview

July's dawn, a chamber's gaze,
Three minds convened, in measured ways.
Gate's firm check, a silent plea,
A journey's start, for all to see.

"Introduce yourself," the Chairman's call,
A tale of study, standing tall.
"Why this role?" a question's art,
Leadership's traits, from mind and heart.

Drills and forces, depths explored,
Teams and projects, wisdom poured.
Casing's shield, and air's command,
A driller's skill, at their hand.

Research's proof, a scholar's claim,
A moment held, in knowledge's flame.
The board's inquiry, keen and bright,
A seeker's path, in dawning light.

12. My Second UPSC INTERVIEW

From gates of youth, to halls of thought,
A seeker's path, with lessons caught.
In coded lines, and research's gleam,
A journey's thread, a vibrant dream.

Through chambers held, where questions rise,
A mind's keen gaze, in wise replies.
In depths of drills, and AI's art,
A striving spirit, and a knowing heart.

From holy rivers, to mountain's crest,
A soul's ascent, in tranquil rest.
In mentors' words, and wisdom's call,
A guiding light, to stand up tall.

Through trials faced, and victories won,
A tapestry woven, 'neath the sun.
In every step, a lesson learned,
A seeker's stride, forever earned.

With open eyes, and spirit free,
To find the truth, for all to see.
In every quest, a deeper grace,
The seeker's journey, time and space.

13. The Scholar's Purse: A Global Tale

From India's shores, where costs are low,
To US heights, where budgets flow.
Europe's balance, a middle ground,
Where knowledge's seeds, are widely found.

A hashtag's plea, for minds to bloom,
Five years of study, dispelling gloom.
In labs and libraries, where wisdom lies,
A scholar's journey, 'neath diverse skies.

Fifty thousand rupees, a monthly grace,
In India's realm, a gentle space.
While dollars soar, to eighty-nine grand,
In stateside halls, a wealthy hand.

Euro's embrace, a thirty-eight's might,
With social shields, and learning's light.
Overheads rise, in varied ways,
A scholar's path, through funding's maze.

Tenfold the gap, 'twixt East and West,
A funding's truth, put to the test.
Joint programs sought, a bridge to span,
Where global minds, together plan.

BITS's vision, a hopeful sign,
International links, where scholars align.
From Pilani's grace, to distant shores,
A scholar's dream, that ever soars.

Let industry's hand, and state's keen eye,
Support the minds, that reach so high.
For knowledge's sake, and progress's call,
To fund the seekers, standing tall.

14. The Architect's Eightfold Path

From vision's seed, a plan takes flight,
Gantt's charted course, in guiding light.
Phase One unfolds, with measured pace,
Scheduling's art, in time and space.

Then voices rise, in customer's plea,
Phase Two's survey, for all to see.
Information's flow, a vital stream,
To shape the product, and fulfill the dream.

Kano's model, in Phase Three's sway,
Classifying needs, to light the way.
Features ranked, with careful hand,
To meet demands, across the land.

Black box's form, in Phase Four's art,
Functional depths, to play their part.
Decomposition's grace, a structured view,
Where every function, shines anew.

House of Quality, in Phase Five's hold,
Problems defined, in stories told.
Quality's function, a guiding star,
To shape the product, near and far.

Morphological thought, in Phase Six's quest,
Concepts born, put to the test.
Critical functions, in patterns bright,
A design's vision, taking flight.

Pugh's matrix shines, in Phase Seven's stage,
Evaluating choices, turning a page.
Quantitative ranks, in measured line,
Selecting concepts, truly divine.

Then Phase Eight's form, the model's grace,
A tangible dream, in time and space.
From planning's seed, to final art,
The architect's journey, a brand new start.

15. The Architect's Code: Mobile and Python's Embrace

A challenge posed, in digital space,
To build a system, with Python's grace.
Automation's dream, in mobile's hand,
A project born, at Pilani's command.

First, needs defined, both strong and clear,
Functional goals, and non-functional gear.
Requirements' core, a vital tree,
Where architecture's roots, for all to see.

Tactics unfold, with measured might,
To conquer ASRs, in day and night.
Five pillars stand, in coded art,
Where performance thrives, and systems start.

Context's scope, in diagrams' frame,
Module's depths, where functions claim.

Components linked, connections bright,
Deployment's form, in digital light.

Python's power, a flowing stream,
Mobile's reach, a vibrant dream.
From coded lines, to user's hand,
Automation's grace, across the land.

In Pilani's halls, where knowledge thrives,
A project's journey, where code survives.
Software's art, in every line,
A digital vision, truly divine.

16. The DevOps Diamond

A purple hue, a golden gleam,
"Best Team" etched, a vibrant dream.
PDC's praise, a shining star,
For those who reached, and went so far.

AWS DevOps, a name held high,
Where dedication touched the sky.
Innovative threads they wove,
Across platforms, systems strove.

Integrations danced,a seamless flow,
Efficiency bloomed, where seeds did sow.
Downtime's shadow, chased away,
By scripts of brilliance, come what may.

Automation's art, a master's hand,
Deployment's speed, across the land.
A team united, strong and bold,
A story of success, to be told.

So let the diamond brightly blaze,
A symbol of their tireless days.
For in their work, a truth we find,
The power of a focused mind.

17. The TCS Gift

Python's weave, AWS's cloud so bright,
Machine Learning's dawn, in guiding light.
TCS's hand, a chance to soar and climb,
A developer's dream, transcending space and time.

US, Mexico's call, a journey's open door,
Mlops' path, where knowledge I explore.
Gratitude's song, within my spirit's core,
For blessings sought, and evermore.

18. Indian Oil Gas and Pipelines: Engineering Solutions

Uganda's lines, where oil and gas would flow,
Caesar's numbers, where stresses start to grow.
A branch's strain, a factor's heavy toll,
One-six-eight's burden, taking its control.

Hangers placed with care, a steady hand,
Eight-six-zero's grace, upon the distant land.
A problem solved, where knowledge found its way,
In pipelines' strength, where progress held its sway.

Sprinkler rings designed, on AutoCAD's bright screen,
One LPM, three LPM, a measured, fluid scene.
Tees of equal measure, reducing's careful art,
API's standards, playing a vital part.

Indian Oil's tanks, where safety found its hold,
ISO angles, stories to be told.

Pressure vessels formed, with ASME's guiding hand,
PVElite's wisdom, across the structured land.

Hoop stress, axial strain, in calculated might,
Thickness, pressure's dance, in day and fading light.
Charpy's impact test, where crashworthiness was weighed,
Explicit dynamics spun, where simulations played.

Creo's shapes, Abaqus' force, where impacts found their form,
Duration's secrets, weathering every storm.
Thickness, material's change, a measured, subtle art,
Validation's truth, where science played its part.

From pipelines' flow, to vessels' mighty frame,
To impact's force, where knowledge earned its name.
A craftsman's skill, in every line and curve,
Where engineering's heart, continues to preserve.

19. New Poem

20. Airless Dreams: The Michelin Tweel's Form

From Pilani's halls, a vision took its flight,
The Michelin Tweel, in structured, airless light.
Customer's voice, through Kano's measured art,
House of Quality's weave, a brand new start.

Black box whispers, morphological's keen eye,
Concepts born from thought, where innovation lie.
Pugh's selection's choice, a guiding, steady hand,
The Tweel's true form, across the waiting land.

Diamond's strength, triangular's bold design,
Creo's shaping grace, where digital lines combine.
Ansys's gaze, where simulations take their hold,
Stress and strain revealed, in stories to be told.

Airless dreams unfold, where rubber meets the road,
A structure born of thought, a heavy burden stowed.
From concept's seed to FEA's measured test,
The Michelin Tweel's form, put knowledge to the best.

21. The Crash's Clock: Charpy's Measured Strike

In Pilani's lab, where impacts found their stage,
Charpy's test unfolded, turning a new page.
Vehicle's safety sought, in crashworthiness's plea,
Where impact's secrets hid, for all the world to see.

FEA's vision cast, in dynamics' explicit sway,
Structural modules hummed, where forces held their way.
Creo's forms defined, Abaqus's strength applied,
As simulations danced, where truths could not hide.

Duration's subtle shift, in thickness's varied line,
Material's change revealed, a measured, clear design.
Computational's tale, with experimental's grace,
Impact energy's truth, in time and measured space.

Validation's hand, where numbers found their creed,
The crash's clock revealed, a necessary deed.
In measured strikes and force, where safety found its

hold,
A story of impact's time, in moments to be told.

38

22. New Poem